AF326715

WHOLENESS *Lifestyle* JOURNAL

allwrite
publishing

" Wholeness lived consistently creates a life and love that does not break. "

CONTENTS

"
Love is not the
foundation of a
healthy relationship,
wholeness is.
"

HOW TO USE THIS
JOURNAL

This journal is not meant to be completed, perfected or used in order. It exists to give your inner world room to speak honestly, imperfectly, and without pressure.

Some pages may remain blank. Others may fill quickly. You might write one sentence, several pages or nothing at all. **All of it is welcome.**

You do not need to answer every question or use every prompt. If a prompt doesn't fit, skip it. If a blank page calls louder, follow that instead. This journal belongs to you.

If you ever feel unsure where to begin, you may return to the prompts in Appendix F of the book. If not, trust what wants to emerge. There is no right way to do this, only an honest one. Whether you use a pencil or pen, write in full sentences or simple phrases, there is no wrong or right way to express yourself as it relates to this journal. There is **only one goal: wholeness!**

"
Whole love is not
something you feel;
it is something you
live.
"

NOTE:
EMOTIONAL
SAFETY & PACING

This journal may bring old memories, emotions or stories to the surface. If at any point you feel overwhelmed, it is okay to stop. **Growth does not require urgency**.

You aren't expected to resolve everything you uncover. Some experiences need to be named before they can be understood, and some truths need time before they make sense.

Move at a pace that honors your emotional and psychological capacity. Take breaks when needed. Reach out for support if something feels too heavy to hold alone.

This isn't about fixing yourself. It's about listening to what's been carried quietly and to what's ready to be acknowledged now.

BROKENNESS vs. WHOLENESS

Brokenness shields you from the truth, allowing you to believe a misconception or lie that you now live with as the truth.

Broken people have allowed these lies to overcome them. Thus, they live as they were never meant to, separated from their true essence and purpose. They are slaves to some destructive belief or feeling that causes them to act and react in unproductive ways, typically hurting themselves or those around them.

Wholeness doesn't mean you're perfect. It means you recognize and reject lies that once hindered you or could be hindering you from the truth of who you are. Will those lies keep trying to return and disrupt your life? Yes, but whole people know what tools to use and how to overcome them.

Brokenness reveals how we lose ourselves in love.
Wholeness reveals how we find ourselves again.

IDENTIFYING
MY
BROKENNESS

What situation, person or group caused you to break? This could include things like a death, divorce, deception, abandonment, disappointment, and so forth.

What aspect of your life reflects this brokenness as a result?
Are you:

Emotionally
Imbalanced

Physically
Diminished

Financially
Irresponsible

Spiritually
Disconnected

Mentally
Confused

Socially
Inept

UNDERSTANDING WHOLENESS

"Wholeness" means being ready to recognize and respond to the truth – both yours and others'. It doesn't mean you're perfect. It means you're willing to address your imperfections with truth and grace.

"We are not meant to be perfect;
we are meant to be whole."

Characteristics of being whole include becoming:

- Honest
- Proactive
- Authentic
- Self-aware
- Courageous
- Confident
- Assertive

The impact of being whole is reflected in your:

- Self-esteem
- Self-respect
- Respect from others
- Confidence
- Focus
- Purpose
- Attraction to what is whole

"Wholeness is when nothing inside you is hiding from the truth anymore."

PART I: THE HEART OF WHOLENESS

This section holds the places where you may have learned to adapt in order to be loved. It is a space for honesty, not self-judgment.

As you write, you may notice patterns, memories or emotions that once helped you survive. Let them be seen without rushing to label or correct them. Focus on you now because wholeness does not begin between two people. It begins within a person.

Write gently. Stop when needed. Let truth surface in its own time.

Reflection: Where in my life do I still feel the need to prove something about myself?

From 1 to 10 (with 10 being your strongest),
how did you do this week in confronting,
challenging or changing your patterns?

____

What contributed to that number?

____

____

What is one step you can take to move forward
this coming week?

____

____

Reflection: What patterns feel familiar in my relationships and how might they have once protected me?

DATE:

From 1 to 10 (with 10 being your strongest),
how did you do this week in confronting,
challenging or changing your patterns?

____

What contributed to that number?

____

____

What is one step you can take to move forward
this coming week?

____

____

Reflection: What part of my story has rarely been spoken out loud?

From 1 to 10 (with 10 being your strongest),
how did you do this week in confronting,
challenging or changing your patterns?

____

What contributed to that number?

____

____

What is one step you can take to move forward
this coming week?

____

____

Reflection: Where have I learned to shrink, perform or stay silent to maintain connection?

DATE:

From 1 to 10 (with 10 being your strongest),
how did you do this week in confronting,
challenging or changing your patterns?

____

What contributed to that number?

____

____

What is one step you can take to move forward
this coming week?

____

____

"Awareness begins when we stop blaming the mirror and start tending to the reflection."

PART II:
A.R.C. OF SELF

This section is about your relationship with yourself, including how you see yourself, treat yourself, and trust your own becoming.

You may notice places where awareness is growing, where respect feels fragile, or where confidence is still forming. None of this needs to be forced. Becoming whole is a process, not a performance.

Let this space support honesty without pressure to change too quickly.

Reflection: What am I becoming more aware of about myself lately?

From 1 to 10 (with 10 being your strongest),
how did you do this week in confronting,
challenging or changing your patterns?

____

What contributed to that number?

____

____

What is one step you can take to move forward
this coming week?

____

____

Reflection: Where do I struggle to honor my own needs, limits or worth?

DATE:

From 1 to 10 (with 10 being your strongest),
how did you do this week in confronting,
challenging or changing your patterns?

____

What contributed to that number?

____

____

What is one step you can take to move forward
this coming week?

____

____

From 1 to 10 (with 10 being your strongest),
how did you do this week in confronting,
challenging or changing your patterns?

____

What contributed to that number?

____

____

What is one step you can take to move forward
this coming week?

____

____

Reflection: What criticism or comment tends to affect me the most, and what might it be revealing about how I see myself?

DATE:

From 1 to 10 (with 10 being your strongest),
how did you do this week in confronting,
challenging or changing your patterns?

____

What contributed to that number?

____

____

What is one step you can take to move forward
this coming week?

____

____

"
Our soul needs are divine in origin, so they are sacred, not selfish.
"

PART III:
SOUL NEEDS

This section invites you to listen beneath behavior and emotion, toward the needs that shape your choices and longings.

Soul needs are not weaknesses. They are signals formed through experience, revealed over time, and honored through discernment.

As you write, allow curiosity to lead. You are not here to diagnose yourself, but to understand yourself more compassionately.

Reflection: What needs seem most alive or
unmet in me right now?

DATE:

Reflection: What needs seem most alive or
unmet in me right now?

From 1 to 10 (with 10 being your strongest),
how did you do this week in confronting,
challenging or changing your patterns?

____

What contributed to that number?

____

____

What is one step you can take to move forward
this coming week?

____

____

Reflection: How have I tried to meet my soul needs in the past and at what cost?

DATE:

From 1 to 10 (with 10 being your strongest),
how did you do this week in confronting,
challenging or changing your patterns?

____

What contributed to that number?

____

____

What is one step you can take to move forward
this coming week?

____

____

From 1 to 10 (with 10 being your strongest),
how did you do this week in confronting,
challenging or changing your patterns?

What contributed to that number?

What is one step you can take to move forward
this coming week?

From 1 to 10 (with 10 being your strongest),
how did you do this week in confronting,
challenging or changing your patterns?

____

What contributed to that number?

____

____

What is one step you can take to move forward
this coming week?

____

____

" Connection
begins where
performance
ends. "

PART IV:
T.O.R.C.H. OF LOVE

This section explores how wholeness is expressed in relationship. As you write, you may reflect on how you connect, protect yourself, or offer yourself to others.

Some reflections here may involve grief, clarity, or boundaries. Let this be a place where truth is named without blame, toward yourself or anyone else.

You are not required to act on everything you see. Awareness itself is meaningful.

Reflection: When do I feel safest being known and when do I tend to hide?

DATE:

From 1 to 10 (with 10 being your strongest),
how did you do this week in confronting,
challenging or changing your patterns?

____

What contributed to that number?

____

____

What is one step you can take to move forward
this coming week?

____

____

From 1 to 10 (with 10 being your strongest),
how did you do this week in confronting,
challenging or changing your patterns?

____

What contributed to that number?

____

____

What is one step you can take to move forward
this coming week?

____

____

From 1 to 10 (with 10 being your strongest),
how did you do this week in confronting,
challenging or changing your patterns?

____

What contributed to that number?

____

____

What is one step you can take to move forward
this coming week?

____

____

From 1 to 10 (with 10 being your strongest),
how did you do this week in confronting,
challenging or changing your patterns?

____

What contributed to that number?

____

____

What is one step you can take to move forward
this coming week?

____

____

"
A whole
relationship
isn't perfect;
it's practiced. "

PART V:
THE PRACTICE OF
WHOLE LOVE

This final section is about integration, moving from awareness to application. We have emphasized the importance of personal growth, but personal growth is not the final destination. It's the foundation for something greater: service.

When two whole individuals come together, they create something larger than themselves. A relationship that supports growth, encourages honesty, and reflects unbroken love through action.

You may reflect on commitments you've made, ones you're reconsidering or new clarity that has emerged. This isn't a place for final answers, but for listening to what feels aligned and true in this season. Let this space hold both hope and honesty.

Reflection: What has shifted in how I understand love, commitment, or wholeness?

From 1 to 10 (with 10 being your strongest),
how did you do this week in confronting,
challenging or changing your patterns?

____

What contributed to that number?

____

____

What is one step you can take to move forward
this coming week?

____

____

From 1 to 10 (with 10 being your strongest),
how did you do this week in confronting,
challenging or changing your patterns?

____

What contributed to that number?

____

____

What is one step you can take to move forward
this coming week?

____

____

From 1 to 10 (with 10 being your strongest),
how did you do this week in confronting,
challenging or changing your patterns?

____

What contributed to that number?

____

____

What is one step you can take to move forward
this coming week?

____

____

Reflection: What am I now willing to make more room for in my relationship (e.g. soul needs, vulnerability, repair)?

From 1 to 10 (with 10 being your strongest),
how did you do this week in confronting,
challenging or changing your patterns?

____

What contributed to that number?

____

____

What is one step you can take to move forward
this coming week?

____

____

FINAL NOTE:
THE WHOLENESS
LIFESTYLE

You may return to these pages whenever needed. If guidance feels helpful, the journal prompts in Appendix F of the book remain available. If silence or introspection feels more truthful, let it lead instead.

Remember, the wholeness lifestyle continues beyond the journal. Wholeness is not a destination or achievement you reach, but a way of relating to yourself, to others, and to God over time.

Reflection: Where are you spiritually, emotionally, psychologically, and physically? Describe your current reality honestly.

DATE:

197